This Jesus Must Die!

A Good Friday
Tenebrae Service

James C. Killough

CSS Publishing Company, Inc., Lima, Ohio

THIS JESUS MUST DIE!

ISBN 0-7880-1128-6   PRINTED IN U.S.A.

*To the members
of Martin Luther Lutheran Church,
Johnson, Nebraska*

Notes On The Service

The focal point of the service is fourteen candles with a larger "Christ Candle" in the middle. As the service progresses the fourteen candles will be extinguished. The "Christ Candle" is never extinguished, symbolizing Christ's never-ending presence.

At the beginning of the service, the light in the worship space should be normal. As the service progresses the worship space will become increasingly dark until by the end of the service only the "Christ Candle" gives any light. *(See the lighting instructions printed throughout the service.)*

As many as fifteen, or as few as two, individuals can effectively lead this service. It will be most effective if a different individual reads each of the seven monologues. The service will take approximately one hour.

Recommended hymns are suggested throughout the service. Other selections can be used in their places. It is recommended that, if possible, the words to the hymns be printed in the bulletin so that the distraction of finding hymns is minimized. Choir selections or other special music can be added.

This Jesus Must Die!

(Lights normal)

OPENING LITANY

L: Were you there when they crucified our Lord?
P: Yes, we were there.
L: Were you there when they nailed him to the tree?
P: Yes, we were there.
L: Were you there when they laid him in the tomb?
P: Yes, we were there.
L: Were you there when they said, "This Jesus must die!"?
P: Yes, we were there.

PRAYER OF PREPARATION and THE LORD'S PRAYER

Lord, at times it causes us to tremble when we consider the sorrow, pain, and suffering you so freely took upon yourself for us. As we follow you to the cross, we can't help but ask why this horrible thing must happen. How is it that the shouts of "hosanna" have so quickly turned to shouts of "crucify him"? But deep down we know. Deep down we know whose sin causes your death. It is our sin, our rejection, our treason that brought you to Calvary. Yes, we were truly there.

We humbly pray that your love, forgiveness, and mercy that so greatly offended us may now be extended to us. Grant that we may die to our sin and so be raised to new life with you. We ask all this, and everything else, in the words you taught us to pray ...

Our Father ...

HYMN   "Beneath The Cross Of Jesus"

THE OFFERING

(Lights subdued, but bright enough to read.)

FIRST SCRIPTURE READING   Luke 19:1-10

(The first candle is extinguished.)

FIRST MONOLOGUE

I'll never forgive Jesus for that. Of all the people he could have stayed with, why Zacchaeus? Of all the inhabitants of Jericho, Zacchaeus was the worst possible choice. Zacchaeus was a traitor, a turncoat; he had sold out to the enemy. And to top it all off, he was getting rich in the process.

You've got to hand it to the Romans, they are as smart as they are cruel. They knew how much we Israelites hated paying their stinking taxes. No one likes taxes. But it's twice as bad when the money goes to the Empire that has conquered your country and now occupies it. And so who do the Romans get to collect their taxes? Do they send in Roman tax collectors? No, they hire our people to do their dirty work for them. And how do they pay these dirty traitors? Tax collectors can charge whatever they can get away with. And after they send in what Rome expects, they get to keep whatever's left, no questions asked.

What sort of people would help the enemy and steal from their own people at the same time? I'll tell you what kind, greedy pigs. Pigs who are out to make an easy buck, even if it means working for the Romans and stealing from your own people. And that's exactly the kind of person Zacchaeus is. Someone who betrayed his own people, happily got rich off their toil and labor, and through it all, helped keep the Romans in power.

And, oh, how rich he became in the process. He admits it himself. He promises to give half of his possessions to the poor and repay all those he's defrauded four times as much. Where do you think he got all that money in the first place?! He got it from us! He's cheated us and robbed us for years while all the time he's lived high and mighty. And now he thinks he can make it all better by giving back part of what he's stolen. He makes me sick. It makes me sick even to think about it.

And now how does he get repaid for all this evil? What's his punishment for selling out his own people? Jesus declares him saved! Of all people, Jesus says salvation has come to Zacchaeus. It isn't right. It isn't fair. Jesus has no right to say Zacchaeus will be saved. Zacchaeus is the worse kind of sinner. Jesus is way out of line. He's really kind of dangerous. Something should be done about him. We can't stand for this. This Jesus must die!

(The second candle is extinguished.)

HYMN   "Alas! And Did My Savior Bleed" verses 1-3

SECOND SCRIPTURE READING   Luke 13:10-17

(The third candle is extinguished.)

SECOND MONOLOGUE

I resent being called a hypocrite. I was just doing my job. I was the leader of the synagogue. I had to say something. I wasn't the one in the wrong. Jesus was the one making trouble.

Now I know what you're thinking. You're thinking all Jesus did was heal this poor woman. How could that be wrong? It's not that Jesus healed her. It's *when* he healed her. He healed her on the Sabbath. Healing is considered work. And work is plainly forbidden on the Sabbath.

Now that's not my idea. I didn't come up with that rule. God did! It's the Third Commandment. "Remember the Sabbath day, and keep it holy. Six days shall you labor and do all your work. But the seventh day is a Sabbath to the Lord your God; you shall not do any work." This Jesus has no right to go around breaking God's commandments whenever he feels like it.

This may sound harsh, but it really isn't. Following God's commandments gives order and structure to our lives. What would

7

happen if people just decided to stop following the Fifth Commandment, "You shall not kill?" Society would fall into chaos. And that's why something as simple as healing on the Sabbath must be stopped. If that kind of thinking spreads, it could lead to all kinds of trouble.

Now don't misunderstand me. I'm not upset that Jesus healed this poor woman. It was a great act of kindness and an impressive demonstration of God's healing power. But not on the Sabbath! Why couldn't he have just waited a few hours to heal her? Soon the Sabbath would have ended, and then everything would have been fine. She'd been this way for eighteen years. Would a few more hours really make any difference? If he had just waited, we could have avoided all this trouble.

But for whatever reason, Jesus didn't wait. He just forged ahead, breaking God's law, ignoring our tradition, making a mockery of our way of life. And not only that, he drove a wedge between those of us in authority and the common people. Those of us with positions of leadership had no choice but to question his acts. It is our job to defend the tradition. But the common people are so swept up in Jesus' teachings and healings, they can't see the larger picture. They don't see how dangerous this Jesus is.

We must put a stop to this. Jesus can't be allowed to continue to cause trouble. He's dangerous. This Jesus must die!

(The fourth candle is extinguished.)

HYMN   "Alas! And Did My Savior Bleed" verses 4 and 5

THIRD SCRIPTURE READING   Luke 6:27-31

(The fifth candle is extinguished.)

THIRD MONOLOGUE

I can't believe this is happening. My teenage son has just come home spouting some new philosophy that's bound to get him into trouble. Those of you who are parents of teenagers will understand what I'm talking about. You know how impressionable teenagers are. They're always excited about whatever's the newest craze, no matter how crazy it is. One of the toughest jobs in the world has got to be raising kids and keeping them on the right track. The last thing we need is some crazy preacher filling our kids' heads with new and revolutionary ideas, especially dangerous ideas. What kind of dangerous ideas, you ask? How about this for starters: Love your enemies, do good to those who hate you, pray for those who abuse you. Can you believe it? That's the kind of ideas my kids are coming home with.

And if that's not bad enough, this crazy preacher is telling my kids that if someone hits them, they should just stand there and get hit a second time. He says if a thief steals your coat, take off your shirt and give that to him as well. And then my favorite: "Give to everyone who begs." Can you believe it? He tells them to give to beggars. There's nothing worse than walking down a big city street and seeing all those beggars. And you know that whatever you give them won't make a bit of difference. It's just like throwing your hard-earned money away. If I've told my children once I've told them a thousand times, give beggars sympathy, not money.

But do they listen to what we teach them? No, they'd rather listen to some preacher who doesn't have anything to give away. They'd rather listen to someone who sums up his philosophy like this: "Do to others as you would have them do to you." Can you believe that? This guy's got it all backwards. It's supposed to be: "Do to others what they do to you." I have no trouble being good to those who are good to me. And that's what I've taught my children. But this idea of loving your enemies and giving without getting back, that's crazy. I don't want my children throwing their lives away. I want my children to be happy and successful. And like it or not, that means you've got to be tough. You've got to watch out for yourself, take what's yours, and fight for your rights.

You know, this really ticks me off. I try to raise my kids to be responsible, successful people and then this Jesus comes along and fills their heads with all sorts of mush. This Jesus is dangerous. Someone should do something about him. We can't just sit around and let him teach our children this kind of stuff. This Jesus must be silenced. This Jesus must die!

(The sixth candle is extinguished.)

HYMN   "Ah, Holy Jesus" verses 1 and 2

FOURTH SCRIPTURE READING   John 8:2-11

(The seventh candle is extinguished.)

FOURTH MONOLOGUE

A gross miscarriage of justice took place that day. I was among the Pharisees who brought that shameful woman to Jesus. We knew it was his custom to go and teach at the Temple, and we were sure we would find him there. And now we finally had a perfect opportunity to clear up all this confusion. It's one thing to talk about forgiving sinners; it's another to deal with a sinner who was caught in the act. We were sure Jesus couldn't weasel his way out of this one. Once and for all we would make him acknowledge that sinners must pay.

Everything was going perfectly at first. The adulterous woman never once denied her guilt, never once even begged for mercy. Like the rest of us, she knew she was wrong. She knew she deserved punishment. God's law must be upheld. Everything was going perfectly.

Even Jesus made no reply at first. He just bent over and started drawing on the ground. At last, the great teacher had nothing to say. There was no way to get out of this one. This woman deserved death, period. When Jesus finally did speak, I thought we had won for sure. He said, "Let anyone among you who is without sin be the first to throw a stone at her." He admitted she deserved death. We had won. Jesus couldn't deny the law this time. I started looking around for a stone to carry out the judgment. It was then that I realized something was wrong.

10

The rest of the scribes and Pharisees looked uncomfortable. I couldn't believe my eyes. They weren't going to let this stop them, were they? We are righteous people. We follow the Law. We make the proper sacrifices. We do what God expects of us. We had every right to judge this woman and then carry out the judgment. We were not caught sinning. She was.

Then things went from bad to worse. Everyone started walking away. These people who had done everything in their power to follow God's law had been chased off by Jesus' trickery. Maybe none of us was completely without sin. Nobody's perfect. But we were surely better than this evil woman before us. It was all I could do to keep from shouting at my colleagues to stop. "What's the matter with all of you?" I wanted to say. "This woman deserves death. Don't let a little case of conscience cloud your judgment. Compared to her, we are without sin." But I said nothing. I just stood there as they all walked away. I finally left too. I couldn't believe this Jesus won again.

Now more than ever I know how much he must be stopped. He can't go on making a mockery of our law and accusing good people of being sinners. He's dangerous. This Jesus must die!

(The eighth candle is extinguished.)

HYMN   "Ah, Holy Jesus" verses 3-5

FIFTH SCRIPTURE READING   Luke 15:11-24

(The ninth candle is extinguished.)

FIFTH MONOLOGUE

This parable wrecked my life. I'm serious, it wrecked my life. Let me tell you how. My father and I were there when Jesus told this parable you call the Prodigal Son. And it was almost as if he was talking about our family. My father has two sons, myself and my younger brother, and the similarities, unfortunately, don't end there. My younger brother is also a wasteful, spoiled, undisciplined good-for-nothing. Of course, it took my father years to admit this. In the beginning Dad always had an excuse for why his little boy didn't measure up. Soon my brother didn't even need to make excuses. Dad would forgive him before he asked. And, of course, I played my part in our little family drama. I was the responsible one. I did my share of the work and my brother's share.

Dad finally did come to his senses. Somehow my father found the courage to admit to himself that this couldn't continue. He knew it wasn't right. And so Dad kicked my brother out. Those were the good days. We hired someone to take his place and for the first time in years the work started getting done. Schedules were met, productivity rose, everything went great. After time, even my father seemed to accept the loss of his son in exchange for efficiency and increased profits.

But then it happened. Jesus came along. My father and I just happened to be there when Jesus was teaching. He started telling parables, one about a lost sheep, a second about a lost coin. And then Jesus started his third parable, "There was a man who had two sons ..." That was the beginning of the end.

When the parable was over, my father was in tears and ran off mumbling something about his poor baby. My father came home late that night. He was half carrying my brother, who was too drunk to walk by himself. Before I could say anything, Dad announced that my brother was home to stay.

That was all two years ago. We went bankrupt a few months after my brother came back home. My father fell sick and soon died because we couldn't afford a doctor. My brother disappeared soon after and I haven't seen him since. And me, I now work for minimum wage on someone else's farm. And all because of Jesus and his parable.

You know, I don't know if my father really even understood what Jesus was getting at in the parable. Jesus was talking about how God treats sinners, not how fathers should treat their sons. It makes me angry every time I think about it. Just look what that kind of thinking did to me. Can you imagine what would happen if God really forgave sinners like that? What was that Jesus thinking?

How could he say such things? Someone should stop him. He's dangerous. This Jesus must die!

(The tenth candle is extinguished.)

HYMN "O Sacred Head, Now Wounded" verses 1 and 2

SIXTH SCRIPTURE READING Mark 14:53-64

(The eleventh candle is extinguished.)

SIXTH MONOLOGUE

For a moment there I thought our case against this Jesus might not hold up. We had lined up so many witnesses to testify against him that surely two of them would agree on some horrible thing he had said or done. But we were having no such luck. None of their testimony was the same. I was afraid we were going to have to let him go. I knew Pilate would not have him executed if we couldn't pin something solid on him and back it up with at least two witnesses. And if ever anyone needed to be killed, Jesus did.

I had been hearing for months about all the trouble he was causing, stirring up the crowds, arguing with the religious authorities, even claiming to be the Messiah. That's exactly what I needed; some would-be Messiah to stir up the masses and start an armed rebellion against Rome. Can you imagine the bloodshed and the destruction, not to mention the religious and political consequences? The last thing I needed was some blaspheming rabble-rouser to mess up everything I had worked for.

But now that we had finally brought him to trial, everything seemed to be slipping away. We were out of witnesses. We had proved nothing. We would have to let him go. I knew I only had one more chance. And I knew it was a long shot. But what other choice did I have? I asked him straight out, "Are you the Messiah, the Son of the Blessed One?" I didn't expect him to answer. I assumed he would just remain silent.

13

I couldn't believe my ears when he answered: "I am; and you will see the Son of Man seated at the right hand of Power and coming with the clouds of heaven." It was more than I could have hoped for in my wildest dreams. Right there in front of everyone he openly admitted to being both Messiah and God's Son. We needed no more evidence. We needed no more witnesses. Pilate would have to do something now. Pilate would have to kill anyone who claimed to be king or God. And this Jesus had just claimed to be both.

Pilate would never know what a favor he was doing me when he sentenced this Jesus to death. Finally all my troubles would be over. Jesus' reputation as a teacher, healer, and miracle worker would slowly fade away. His ragtag followers would disband. And all this nonsense would come to an end. Order would be restored. Jesus has caused enough trouble. Someone has to do something about it. He's dangerous. He has to be stopped. He has to be silenced. There's no doubt about it, this Jesus must die!

(The twelfth candle is extinguished.)

HYMN   "O Sacred Head, Now Wounded" verses 3 and 4

(At this time all the lights should be turned off.)

SEVENTH SCRIPTURE READING   Luke 23:32-49

(The thirteenth candle is extinguished.)

SEVENTH MONOLOGUE

Can you believe this guy? Even as he hangs on the cross dying, he extends God's grace and mercy to those who don't deserve it. Who is he to say: "Truly I tell you, today you will be with me in Paradise"? Doesn't he get it? Doesn't he realize that's exactly the kind of talk that got him crucified? We have had enough of his offering God's grace and mercy to the undeserving. He can't be allowed to continue forgiving sinners like that.

14

What about us? What about us good religious people? What about those of us who try as hard as we can to do what God expects of us? We might not be perfect, but at least we try. Don't we deserve something for at least trying? I hate to admit it, but I resent the fact that Jesus freely offers sinners what I have worked so hard to earn.

Now I understand why so many people thought Jesus must die. His notion of God's forgiveness really is offensive to those of us who try our best to earn God's salvation. And I always assumed bad people thought Jesus must die.

(Pause)

All of a sudden, that other thing Jesus said from the cross makes sense. "Father, forgive them; for they know not what they are doing." I never thought the "they" included me. It makes you wonder if we're as good as we think we are. We obviously need as much forgiveness as anyone else Jesus forgave.

But it's too late now. Jesus is crucified. He's dead and buried. Without knowing it, we put to death the one God sent to save us. But we can't undo what we've done. It's out of our hands. I guess it's all up to God now.

(The fourteenth candle is extinguished.)

HYMN   "Were You There" verses 1-3

(The final hymn "Were You There" is probably familiar and repetitive enough that it can be sung in the dark without reading the words. After the fourteenth candle has been extinguished, leaving only the "Christ Candle" lit, announce the opening lines of each verse of the hymn: "We will now sing 'Were you there when they crucified my Lord?'; 'Were you there when they nailed him to the tree?'; 'Were you there when they laid him in the tomb?' ")

(Depart in silence.)

www.ingramcontent.com/pod-product-compliance
Lightning Source LLC
Chambersburg PA
CBHW070044040426
42331CB00033B/2504